We Use Numbers

by Margie Burton, Cathy French, and Tammy Jones

Table of Contents

How Do We Use Numbers at Home?

We use numbers at home.

My mom uses numbers in the kitchen when she bakes.

Sometimes I help her.

We measure the flour, sugar,
and milk when we make a cake.
The numbers tell us how much to put in.

We use numbers when we turn the oven on
to bake the cake.

We use numbers to see how long the cake
should stay in the oven.

My dad uses numbers in his workroom.
He is making a home for our dog.
Sometimes I help him, too.

He uses numbers when he measures the wood.
The numbers tell him where he should cut
the wood.

He uses numbers when he counts how many nails
to put in.

Every morning my mom and dad use numbers
to find the weather show on TV.

The numbers on the show help them know
what the weather will be like that day.

Forecast For Friday

1:12:12 PM
THU FEB 10

Las Vegas
58°

Bakersfield
59°

Flagstaff
35°

Dagget

Los Angeles
63°

Palm Springs
67°

Phoenix
65°

San Diego
63°

Yuma
70°

Temp: 63°F

I use numbers at home, too.
I use numbers to dial the telephone
to call my grandma and grandpa.

Grandma & Grandpa Martinez
629 Fifth Avenue
Pelham, NY 10803

I use numbers when I write them a letter, too.
The numbers in their address help the mailman
find their house.

How Do We Use Numbers at School?

We use numbers at school, too.

We look at the numbers
on the clock to know when it
is time to go to class.

We use numbers to find our room.

My teacher uses numbers when
she counts to see how many children
are at school that day.

She also uses numbers when
she counts the lunch money.

We learn all about numbers during math time.
I like math. Math is fun.

We use numbers when we play outside.

We use numbers every day. They tell
us many things.

What do these numbers tell us?